T0009995

ELIZABETH
BLACKWELL

ELIZABETH
BLACKWELL
TRAILBLAZING WOMAN DOCTOR

MATT DOEDEN

LERNER PUBLICATIONS ◆ MINNEAPOLIS

Copyright © 2022 by Lerner Publishing Group, Inc.

All rights reserved. International copyright secured. No part of this book may be reproduced, stored in a retrieval system, or transmitted in any form or by any means—electronic, mechanical, photocopying, recording, or otherwise—without the prior written permission of Lerner Publishing Group, Inc., except for the inclusion of brief quotations in an acknowledged review.

Lerner Publications Company
An imprint of Lerner Publishing Group, Inc.
241 First Avenue North
Minneapolis, MN 55401 USA

For reading levels and more information, look up this title at www.lernerbooks.com.

Image credits: FLHC 1111/Alamy Stock Photo, p. 2; Library of Congress (LC-USZ62-57850), p. 6; Peter Steiner/Alamy Stock Photo, p. 8; Library of Congress (LC-DIG-ppmsc-08051), p. 9; N. d. Natur gez. v. Walter Ochs; Lith. Anst. v. Walter Ochs & Co., Magdeburg/Wikimedia Commons, p. 11; Everett Collection/Shutterstock.com, pp. 12, 33, 34; Grafissimo/Getty Images, p. 13; Library of Congress, Prints & Photographs Division, Farm Security Administration/Office of War Information Black-and-White Negatives, p. 15; maodesign/Getty Images, p. 16; Library of Congress, Manuscript Division, Blackwell Family Papers, p. 17 (left, right); pictore/Getty Images, p. 18; 100/Getty Images, p. 19; Andrew Markham/Wikimedia Commons (CC 4.0), p. 21; AP Photo, pp. 22, 24; decade3d/Getty Images, p. 23; Courtesy of the National Library of Medicine, p. 25; Wikimedia Commons, p. 27; Pictorial Press Ltd/Alamy Stock Photo, p. 28; Library of Congress, Prints & Photographs Division, Detroit Publishing Company Collection, p. 29; The History Collection/Alamy Stock Photo, p. 30; John Parrot/Stocktrek Images/Getty Images, p. 31; ilbusca/Getty Images, p. 32; Library of Congress (LC-USZ62-61779), p. 35; Everett Collection Inc/Alamy Stock Photo, p. 36; Colport/Alamy Stock Photo, p. 37; agefotostock/Alamy Stock Photo, p. 39; John Minchillo/Photographer, p. 40; Elizabeth Blackwell Historic Plaque Unveiling Ceremony/Wikimedia Commons (CC 2.0), p. 41. Cover: Pictorial Press Ltd/Alamy Stock Photo.

Main body text set in Rotis Serif Std 55 Regular. Typeface provided by Adobe Systems.

Library of Congress Cataloging-in-Publication Data

Names: Doeden, Matt, author.
Title: Elizabeth Blackwell: trailblazing woman doctor / Matt Doeden.
Description: Minneapolis: Lerner Publications, [2022] | Series: Gateway biographies | Includes
    bibliographical references and index. | Audience: Ages 9-14 | Audience: Grades 7-9 |
    Summary: "Elizabeth Blackwell shattered the glass ceiling as the first woman doctor.
    Learn how she defied stereotypes and opened a medical practice to treat female patients"
    —Provided by publisher.
Identifiers: LCCN 2020042745 (print) | LCCN 2020042746 (ebook) | ISBN 9781728404486
    (library binding) | ISBN 9781728418162 (ebook)
Subjects: LCSH: Blackwell, Elizabeth, 1821-1910. | Women physicians—Biography—Juvenile
    literature. | Women in medicine—History—Juvenile literature.
Classification: LCC R154.B623 D64 2022 (print) | LCC R154.B623 (ebook) | DDC 610.82—dc23

LC record available at https://lccn.loc.gov/2020042745
LC ebook record available at https://lccn.loc.gov/2020042746

Manufactured in the United States of America
2-52456-49020-2/22/2022

TABLE OF CONTENTS

A portrait of
Elizabeth Blackwell

On a November day in 1847, twenty-six-year-old Elizabeth Blackwell began a voyage that would change her life—and medicine in the United States—forever. For years, Blackwell had fought to gain admission to a medical university. At the time, all doctors were men. But she was ready to change that.

Rejection after rejection had piled up. Some people told her that women couldn't be doctors because they lacked the ability or they couldn't compete with men. Others said that women would never complete the difficult training. Even those who supported Blackwell told her it might be impossible. They suggested she travel to Europe and dress as a man. It was, they said, the only way she could hope to get the education she wanted.

Geneva University

But Blackwell wanted to be accepted for herself. Her dedication paid off when she was admitted to Geneva University in Geneva, New York. She didn't waste any time preparing, and within two weeks she was on her way to the university.

When she arrived, she dove into her studies. She listened to lectures on medicine and anatomy. She dissected animals, learning the precise cuts of a surgeon. Blackwell loved the hard work and late nights studying. She wrote to her sister, describing her studies and experience. "The weather is still gloomy," she wrote. "But I feel sunshiny and happy, strongly encouraged with a grand future before me."

A CURIOUS CHILD

Elizabeth Blackwell was born on February 3, 1821, in Bristol, England. She was the third of nine children born to her parents, Samuel and Hannah Blackwell. She lived with her parents, her siblings, and four of her aunts in Bristol. There, Samuel Blackwell owned and operated a successful sugar refinery.

Elizabeth's earliest memories were of being with her two older sisters, Anna and Marian. She loved to play with them in the family's gardens. She recalled gazing through Anna's telescope at distant houses and gardens. She once asked her aunt to let her take the telescope to the roof for a better view. But her aunt was worried about her safety and denied her request.

Elizabeth was born in Bristol, England.

While she was growing up, boys and girls were often treated much differently. Education was expensive. Many families could not afford it for all of their children. So families often chose to educate only their boys. But not the Blackwells. Because of Samuel Blackwell's refinery business, they had enough money to educate all of their children. Her parents wanted Elizabeth and her sisters to have all the advantages that their boys had. They taught Elizabeth to think for herself. Elizabeth studied math, science, and literature with tutors.

"Only on rare occasions did any of the children go to school," Elizabeth wrote in her autobiography. "Governesses and masters at home supplied the necessary book knowledge; and a passion for reading grew up, which made the present of a new book the greatest delight, and our own pocket-money was chiefly spent in buying books."

Elizabeth found that her family's morals and her family's livelihood were in disagreement. Her family was against slavery. But her father did business with companies that enslaved people. His sugar refinery relied on sugarcane that had been harvested by forced labor through slavery. Wanting to speak out against the sugar industry's reliance on slavery, Elizabeth and her siblings gave up eating sugar.

Life in Bristol changed around 1828. A fire destroyed her father's sugar refinery. He chose not to rebuild it. He sensed a growing unrest in England over too few people having the right to vote and the government refusing

A refinery similar to Samuel Blackwell's

reforms that would make voting more accessible. That, combined with an outbreak of the disease cholera, pushed him to make a change.

In August 1832, Elizabeth and her family packed their belongings and boarded the ocean liner *Cosmo*. Their seven-week voyage to New York was not easy. Cholera was aboard the ship, and several passengers died along the way. But the Blackwells, whose wealth allowed them to stay in a less crowded part of the ship than lower-class passengers, avoided infection. After arriving to the United States, they stepped off the ship and into New York City, ready to begin a new life.

ADVENTURE AND TRAGEDY

Her father started a new sugar refinery in New York.
Elizabeth attended school, where she became more and
more active in the antislavery movement. The Blackwells
welcomed leaders of the movement into their home. One
of them was the Reverend Samuel H. Cox. Cox's life
had been threatened after he claimed that Jesus of the
Christian Bible had not been a white man. The Blackwells
took him in and gave him refuge.

The family spent six years in New York City and
nearby Jersey City, New Jersey. In 1838, when Elizabeth
was seventeen years old, they moved again. This time,
they headed west by
stagecoach, to the growing
town of Cincinnati,
Ohio. For Elizabeth, the
voyage was an amazing
adventure. "We left New
York full of hope and
eager anticipation," she
wrote. "We were delighted
with the magnificent
scenery of the mountains
and rivers as we crossed
Pennsylvania. . . . With
eager enjoyment of
the new scenes, the
prosperous little Western
town was reached."

*At the time, stagecoaches traveled
about 12 miles (19 km) per hour.
That means it would have taken
the Blackwells about fifty-two
hours to reach Cincinnati.*

Moving to Cincinnati was a big change for Elizabeth.

The scenery wasn't the only change. Elizabeth quickly noticed how different the people were in Ohio. In New York, people had behaved much as they had back in England. She referred to New York and England as an older society that followed certain rules of social conduct. Cincinnati was more of a frontier town, without the wealthy families of England and New York, and its people came with a way of life more tied to survival than to social codes. Their different ways of looking at the world struck young Elizabeth.

But then tragedy struck. After the move, her father grew ill with a fever. His health rapidly declined, and he died on August 7, 1838. It was a terrible blow to the Blackwells. They mourned the loss of their father, who had led the family from England to New York to Ohio. And with him gone, they found themselves without any income. Elizabeth had lived most of her life in comfort, based on the money he earned. Suddenly, that was gone. Just earning enough money to survive became the focus of her life.

"The irreparable loss completely altered our lives," she wrote. "Recovering from the first effects of the stunning blow, we began to realize our position." Elizabeth, Anna, and Marian immediately set up a boarding school for young women. "For the next few years, until the younger children grew up and were able to gradually share in the work," Elizabeth wrote, "we managed to support the family and maintain a home."

Setting up the school with her sisters was just the start of Elizabeth's passion for women's education. Even in the wealthier and more progressive societies of Bristol and New York, many did not take women's education seriously. That was even more true in Cincinnati. She joined the fight for more education for women. Meanwhile, she took a growing interest in politics. She supported progressive candidates who fought for broader rights for all, including the abolition of slavery.

STRIKING OUT

In 1842 Blackwell and her sisters closed their school. Their younger siblings had grown, and the older sisters were looking for a change. At first, Blackwell continued teaching some of her pupils privately. But then she was offered a job running a school in Henderson, Kentucky. She took it.

She was in for a culture shock. Kentucky was tobacco-growing country. The industry relied heavily on the forced labor of slavery. All her life, Blackwell had

A field of tobacco plants

been a vocal abolitionist. In Kentucky she saw slavery firsthand. "I dislike slavery more and more every day," she wrote in a letter to her family.

Yet even as she spoke against slavery, Blackwell held racist views. She seemed to look down on enslaved people. Blackwell was simultaneously prejudiced and pro-abolition, believing that no human should be enslaved. She said, "I suppose I see it here in its mildest form . . . but to live in the midst of beings degraded to the utmost in body and mind . . . [and] be utterly unable to help them, is to me dreadful."

Blackwell ran the small school for only a short time. The injustice of slavery weighed heavily on her. She resigned after just one term of teaching. It was time to try something new.

Blackwell returned to Ohio. She studied German, music, and other subjects on her own. During this time, one of her friends suggested that she should study medicine. The friend, a woman who was in poor health, suggested that a female doctor would make her far more comfortable and take her concerns more seriously than the male doctors she saw.

At first, Blackwell was uncertain about the suggestion. She wasn't interested in medicine, and the idea of treating people did not appeal to her. "The very thought of dwelling on the physical structure of the body and its various ailments filled me with disgust," she wrote.

A doctor treating a patient at home in 1896

Blackwell wrote many letters to friends and family, including these two.

Yet the idea stuck with Blackwell. The more she thought about it, the more the idea grew on her. She knew she could make a difference by treating others. She asked the doctors she knew about how she could become a doctor. Everyone she asked told her the same thing. It was impossible. A woman could not go to medical school.

The more people told Blackwell that she couldn't become a doctor, the more determined she became to do it. "The idea of winning a doctor's degree [became] a great moral struggle," she wrote, "and the moral fight possessed immense attraction for me."

Blackwell's mind was made up. She was going to become a doctor, no matter what it took.

In the 1800s, most schools were only one room.

CHASING THE DREAM

Obstacles remained between Blackwell and a medical degree. The first challenge was earning money to pay for the education she would need. So she took a job teaching in Asheville, North Carolina, and began saving money. She was careful in which job she took, however. She wanted to do more than just earn money. She also wanted to get a head start on her studies. Blackwell took a position at a school whose principal, John Dickson, was a former doctor. She took a room in his house and spent much of her free time reading his library of medical books. Dickson supported Blackwell's dream, and the two discussed a range of topics, including medicine. The Dickson family even gave their guest a nickname—Dr. Blackwell.

Blackwell was generally happy during her time in Asheville. But the issues of racism and slavery continued to gnaw at her. When she tried to teach Black children to read, she was quickly stopped. State law forbid teaching people of color to read. But Blackwell created a Sunday school for people who were enslaved.

Blackwell never lost sight of her medical dreams. In 1846 the Asheville school closed. Blackwell traveled to Charleston, South Carolina, where she taught at a boarding school while studying with John Dickson's brother, Samuel Dickson, a practicing doctor. Meanwhile, she wrote letters to medical schools, searching for placement. The letters didn't work. So in 1847, Blackwell headed to Philadelphia, Pennsylvania, a center for medical schools, ready to ask in person.

Blackwell began reading medical books like this one.

Blackwell made her way to all the Philadelphia medical schools. She made her case to professors. One professor laughed at her when she told him her goals. But she pressed on, and slowly, she won him over. It wasn't enough, though. Even as she gained support from people at medical schools, every door she tried for admittance remained closed.

But Blackwell was determined to find an opening. She didn't want just to become a doctor. She wanted to create a path for more people in the United States to do so. She wrote, "It was to my mind a moral crusade on which I had entered, a course of justice and common sense, and it must be pursued in the light of day . . . to accomplish its end."

None of the big medical schools in Philadelphia accepted Blackwell. So she looked at smaller schools. Once again, the rejections piled up. But finally, Blackwell received the news she had been waiting for. On October 20, 1847, Geneva University in western New York accepted Blackwell's application. Her long search was over.

Blackwell wasted no time. On November 4, she left Philadelphia for Geneva. She began taking classes as soon as she arrived several days later.

DEEP IN STUDY

It was an exciting time in Blackwell's life. Her life centered on her studies. She didn't want anything to distract her from her goals.

GENEVA UNIVERSITY

Geneva University, also called Geneva College or Geneva Medical College, was founded in 1834 in Geneva, New York. When the university got Blackwell's application, the staff did not know what to do. Many of the staff opposed admitting her. But no one would make a decision. Instead, they allowed the college's 150 male students to vote. The students chose to accept Blackwell. Some of the students may have intended their acceptance of Blackwell as a joke, but Blackwell didn't care. It was the chance she needed.

Geneva University is now called Hobart and William Smith Colleges.

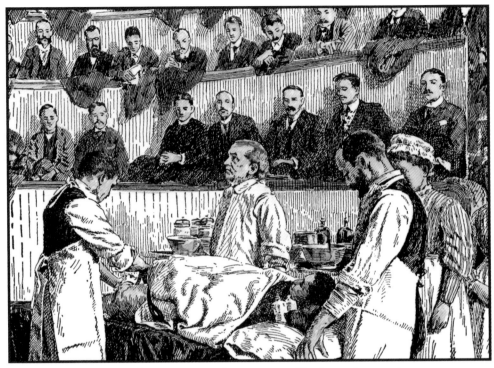

Doctors perform a procedure as medical students observe.

Blackwell was changing the way people thought about the medical profession. At first, she didn't realize the full impact of her presence. "I had not the slight idea of the commotion created by my appearance as a medical student in the little town," she wrote. "Very slowly I perceived that . . . ladies stopped to stare at me, as at a curious animal. . . . Feeling the unfriendliness of the people . . . I never walked abroad. . . . I knew when I shut the great doors [at the school] behind me that I shut out all kindly criticism, and I soon felt perfectly at home amongst my fellow students."

After finishing finals, Blackwell was ready to keep moving forward. She spent the summer break observing and working at a hospital in Philadelphia. There, she still experienced sexism. Some of the doctors didn't support Blackwell and her medical dreams. Some would leave a room if she entered or would stop working if she came in to observe. She focused on learning from those who would teach her.

In September 1848, Blackwell returned to Geneva. At the time, a group of diseases called typhus, or typhoid fever, raged through parts of the world. Blackwell was interested in the disease and its treatment. Like all medical students at Geneva, Blackwell needed to write a thesis—an in-depth research paper—to graduate. She chose to write hers on typhus. Blackwell focused on how the disease spread, including that the poor were at the greatest risk, due to living in unsanitary conditions. Her thesis earned praise at the National Medical Convention held in Boston, Massachusetts.

Salmonella typhi *is the bacteria that causes typhoid fever.*

Blackwell's hard work paid off. She completed her studies and accepted her medical degree on January 23, 1849. At the graduation ceremony, inside a local church, she and her fellow students stepped up one at a time to accept their degrees. Blackwell's turn finally came. Wearing a black silk dress and cape, with her hair in braids, she stepped forward. The room fell silent as the university's president handed her the diploma.

"I thank you sir," Blackwell said as she accepted the degree. "It shall be the effort of my life . . . to shed honor on this Diploma."

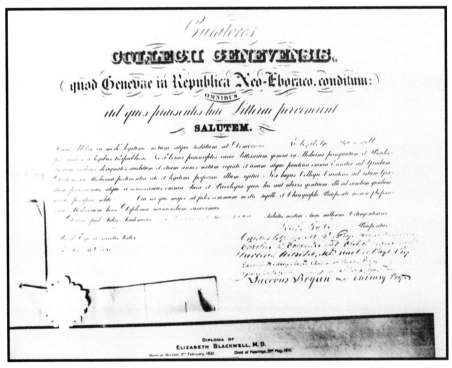

An image of Blackwell's diploma from Geneva University

Though Blackwell faced challenges, she was grateful for her time at La Maternité.

Later, during the ceremony, speaker Dr. Charles Lee called attention to Blackwell and the audience erupted in applause. She had just become the first woman in the United States to earn a medical degree. Her achievement allowed others to follow in her footsteps, including her younger sister, Emily, who earned her medical degree from Medical College of Cleveland, Ohio, in 1854.

In April 1849, Blackwell traveled to Europe to practice as a doctor in a hospital and continue learning. Hospitals refused to accept her as a practicing doctor due to her gender. When Blackwell was finally admitted to La Maternité—a hospital for women giving birth—they did not accept her as a doctor. Instead, she became a student midwife, a person who helps in delivering babies. Regardless, Blackwell said her hands-on training at La Maternité was very valuable.

In November 1849 she was treating a baby who had an eye infection. She used a syringe to draw infected fluid from the eye, and some of the fluid splattered into her own left eye.

By the evening, her eye was swollen and infected. Another doctor tried to treat the infection with the tools of the day. They tried to burn the infection away with heat. They applied leeches to suck blood and fluid from the eye. Yet the infection grew worse, and Blackwell grew more and more concerned.

"For three days this continued," Blackwell wrote. "Then the disease had done its worst. . . . Ah! How dreadful it was to find the daylight gradually fading . . . and the eye was left in darkness."

The infection left Blackwell blind in her left eye. Surgeons removed the eye. She understood that her hopes to become a surgeon one day had been dashed. Keen eyesight was critical to performing surgery, and the loss of her vision in one eye closed that door to her. It was hard for Blackwell to accept at first. But she realized that her vision was one part of her and didn't define her. She continued moving forward with her medical career.

CAREER AND FAMILY

After she recovered, Blackwell studied in London, England. She befriended Florence Nightingale, a young nurse who went on to revolutionize nursing by helping

Florence Nightingale was a social reformer who created modern nursing.

to formalize training for nurses and making the job a profession. But Blackwell found that sexism in London was just as bad or worse than it was in the United States. So in 1851, she returned to the United States. She went to New York to begin her own medical practice.

As usual, obstacles stood in her way. Many people were hesitant to see a female doctor. Her practice struggled. In addition to owning her own practice, Blackwell became a prolific author of medical papers. Blackwell's papers often focused on the mental and emotional parts of health. Her first paper, published in 1852, was *The Laws of Life; with Special Reference to the Physical Education of Girls.*

Blackwell continued to look for her place. She applied at the women's department of a medical clinic, called a dispensary. The clinic rejected her. They wouldn't hire a female doctor. So instead, Blackwell continued making her own way and formed her own clinic, the New York Dispensary for Poor Women and Children, in 1854. Her plan was to hire women. She wanted to make opportunities for those that were coming up behind her. Blackwell knew the prejudice she experienced and wanted to make an easier path for other women to practice medicine.

Blackwell focused on treating poor immigrant communities. People in these communities often lived in places with poor sanitation, no hot water, and no indoor

A female doctor treating a patient in 1865

Blackwell helped people living in New York adopt more healthful lifestyles.

toilets. Diseases—including typhus—spread quickly in these communities. Blackwell offered her services for free. Several members of the religious group called Quakers funded the small clinic.

Blackwell believed that lifestyle greatly impacted health. She went into poor neighborhoods to teach people about hygiene, sanitation, and a healthful diet. She believed that good habits were even more important to fighting disease than medicine, and she did all she could to spread that message.

Although her medical career was finally taking off, Blackwell was struggling in her personal life. More and more, she was feeling isolated and lonely. She needed something more than just her career. In 1854 she adopted seven-year-old Katherine Barry, known as Kitty, from a nearby orphanage.

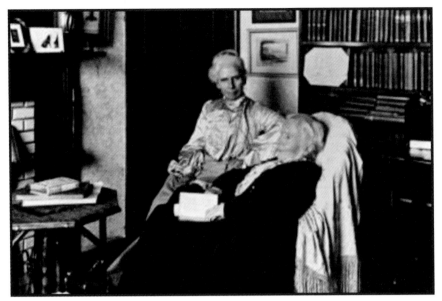

Blackwell (right) and Barry (left) in their home in 1905

"I feel full of hope and strength for the future," Blackwell wrote in her diary shortly after adopting Kitty. "I desperately needed the change of thought she compelled me to give her. It was a dark time, and she did me good. . . . Now I look forward with much hope to the coming events of the year."

The match was good for both of them. The two developed a close bond, and Kitty remained by Blackwell's side into adulthood.

In 1858 Blackwell returned to England with her daughter. She hoped to set up a clinic in London that was similar to the one she'd started in New York. At the time, England still didn't allow female doctors. But because of a law that recognized foreign doctors, she was included on the British medical register. That made her England's first official female doctor.

THE CIVIL WAR

Through her career, Blackwell never forgot the fight to end slavery. By the late 1850s and early 1860s, the topic divided the country. Northern states generally supported abolition. Southern states wanted slavery to continue.

In 1860 Abraham Lincoln was elected president. He received heavy support in the North and deep opposition in the South. Many in the South were furious.

Lincoln took office on March 4, 1861. A little more than a month later, the American Civil War (1861–1865) began. Southern states fought to leave the Union and form a new nation, the Confederate States of America.

Union and Confederate troops fight during the Battle of Opequon.

Northern states, or the Union, fought to keep the nation whole and end slavery.

As an abolitionist, Blackwell was keenly interested in the outcome of the war. She said, "To us, nourished from childhood on the idea of human freedom and justice, the [war] became of absorbing interest. . . . We threw ourselves energetically into the cause of freedom."

As the fighting began and soldiers were wounded and killed, the need for medical support grew. Blackwell helped to run the Women's Central Relief Association, which later became part of the United States Sanitary Commission. The organization helped to train nurses

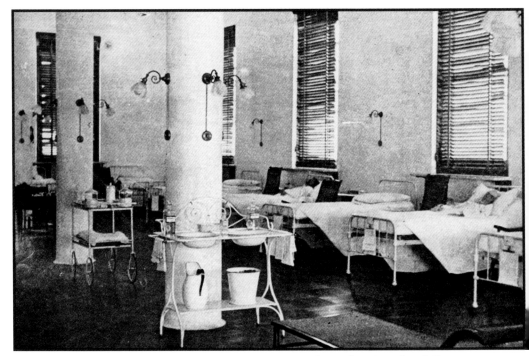

A military hospital used to treat sick and injured soldiers

Abraham Lincoln served as US president from 1861-1865.

to work on the battlefield. She worked closely with Dorothea Dix, superintendent of army nurses for the Union army, to teach as many capable nurses as she could. Dix was a major figure in medical reform in the United States at the time. She fought for greater care for underserved populations, including those experiencing mental illness and Indigenous peoples.

Blackwell was a big help to the Union. In 1864 Lincoln even invited her to meet him at the White House. Blackwell described the president in a letter to her daughter: "A tall, ungainly loose-jointed man was standing in the middle of the room. He came forward with a pleasant smile and shook hands with us. I should not at all have recognized him from the photographs. . . . Then he plumped his long body down on the corner of the large table . . . and began to discuss some point about the war."

The terribly bloody war killed or wounded more than 1.5 million people. In 1865 the Confederate forces surrendered. The Union had won. Slavery officially ended with the adoption of the Thirteenth Amendment later that year.

NEW FIGHTS

The 1860s was a time of political change and scientific change. Vaccines were coming into widespread use. Doctors injected small amounts of a disease into patients. The body's immune system reacted by creating antibodies to fight off the disease. The vaccines were not as safe as modern vaccines are. The science was new, and doctors were still learning how to make the injections safe.

In the late 1860s, Blackwell vaccinated a baby against a disease. The baby reacted badly to the injection. Despite her best efforts, the child died. Blackwell called it the most painful experience of her medical career and remained a critic of vaccinations for the rest of her life.

Louis Pasteur created a reliable vaccination process.

More than a decade later, advances in vaccine science made by Louis Pasteur made vaccinations much safer. But Blackwell refused to change her mind on the subject, even in the face of new science.

In 1868, Blackwell helped create the Women's Medical College of the New York Infirmary. The medical college for women operated next to the infirmary. As a four-year college, it was one of the first schools in the United States to require

The Women's Medical College of the New York Infirmary was the first college to offer extensive medical training for women.

extended training. The college went on to become part of Weill Cornell Medicine.

Blackwell left the dispensary in 1869, leaving her sister Emily in charge. She was ready to tackle a new challenge. She returned to England.

There, Blackwell became involved in politics. She joined a movement to overturn the Contagious Diseases Act, a British law that forced some women to undergo invasive medical examinations. She also worked to set up education for women. In 1874 she teamed with doctor and teacher Sophia Jex-Blake to set up the London

At the London School of Medicine for Women,
students received hands-on training.

School of Medicine for Women. Blackwell became a
professor and chair of the gynecology department.
Gynecology is the medical study of women's
reproductive organs. Blackwell stayed at the London
School of Medicine for Women until her retirement at
the age of eighty-six in 1907.

Blackwell also helped form the British National Health
Society. It focused on teaching people ways to prevent the
spread of diseases. The society's motto was that prevention
is better than a cure. These lessons were offered free
so that everyone could benefit from them. The classes
taught women how to work as health visitors—people who
promote good health and prevent illness.

EMILY BLACKWELL

Blackwell wasn't the only doctor in the family. Her younger sister, Emily Blackwell, followed in her footsteps, becoming the third woman in the United States to earn a medical degree.

Emily Blackwell, born in 1826, tried to follow her sister to Geneva University. But they refused to accept women after Elizabeth Blackwell graduated, even though she had graduated at the top of her class. Instead, the younger Blackwell studied at Medical College of Cleveland, Ohio. She earned her medical degree in 1854. She helped her sister found the dispensary in 1856 and remained with the clinic for forty years.

Emily Blackwell was a medical professor, a surgeon, a gynecologist, and an obstetrician.

She lived with her partner Elizabeth Cushier, another doctor who also worked at the clinic. Emily Blackwell died on September 7, 1910, just a few months after her older sister died.

LATER YEARS AND DEATH

With her days of practicing medicine behind her, Blackwell turned her attention to spiritual and moral issues. She had never strongly associated with any church. But she was outspoken about her religious beliefs. She became one of the leaders of the Christian Socialist Movement. This group believed in justice, mercy, and the theory that everyone is connected. As a part of this movement, she argued against the growing belief that science and religion were not consistent with each other. She believed that religious morals played a key role in medicine.

Blackwell also continued to speak out against much of the time's evolving medical science. Doctors and scientists were gaining a better understanding of how germs, including bacteria, caused disease. Blackwell didn't believe it. She thought that germs only played a small role, and that doctors were ignoring larger moral and spiritual issues.

History has proved some of Blackwell's ideas to be incorrect. Germs do cause disease. Vaccines are safe. But in other beliefs, she was ahead of her time. She promoted hygiene and healthful living. She said that mental and spiritual well-being were important parts of a person's overall health. She argued for the equality of all women and pushed for more widespread sexual education. And she paved many paths for women to join the medical profession.

In 1895, at the age of seventy-four, Blackwell wrote and published her autobiography, *Pioneer Work in*

*A portrait of Blackwell
reading*

Opening the Medical Profession to Women. In it, she traced her life and her pursuit of a career that had been off-limits to her. She also outlined her vision of the future, in which men and women work together as equals.

After the publication of her autobiography, Blackwell continued to lecture but started to step back from public life. She spent much of her time traveling. She took a trip to Scotland and also revisited the United States.

A LASTING LEGACY

Blackwell's clinic started with a single room. In the 150 years since she opened it, it has grown and grown. Its name, location, and mission have changed several times, but the hospital has remained in operation ever since. Since 2013 its name has been NewYork-Presbyterian Lower Manhattan Hospital. The modern hospital has about 130 beds and serves the Lower Manhattan region of New York City.

"Dr. Blackwell's legacy lives on in our hospital," said Juan Mejia, senior vice president and chief operating officer of the hospital. "Her social consciousness lives on in our commitment to women and children and the diverse and vibrant communities that we serve. And her leadership lives on in our women physician leaders making a difference here at NewYork-Presbyterian Lower Manhattan Hospital."

The NewYork-Presbyterian Lower Manhattan Hospital still embraces Blackwell's values.

A plaque is unveiled in 2018 honoring Blackwell and her work on the New York Dispensary for Poor Women and Children.

Blackwell died of a stroke on May 31, 1910, in the English town of Hastings. Her ashes were buried in Kilmun, Scotland. Blackwell's obituary, printed in the *British Medical Journal*, celebrated her achievements. "It was, indeed, her womanly character, coupled with her intense earnestness, which mainly enabled her to overcome the difficulties in her path," it read. "Although she appears to have turned to medicine with some reluctance in the first place, she soon acquired a belief that she had a definite 'call,' and retained this belief to the end."

IMPORTANT DATES

1821   Blackwell is born in Bristol, England, on February 3.

1832   The Blackwell family sails to the United States.

1838   The Blackwell family moves to Cincinnati, Ohio. Her father, Samuel Blackwell, dies soon after the move.

1844   Blackwell travels to Kentucky to take a teaching job.

1847   Blackwell is accepted to Geneva University, where she becomes a medical student.

1848   Blackwell completes her thesis on the disease typhus.

1849   Blackwell becomes the first woman in the United States to earn her medical degree.

        She travels to Europe.

1854   Blackwell opens a clinic in New York City, the New York Dispensary for Poor Women and Children.

Blackwell adopts a daughter, Katherine Barry.

1861   The American Civil War begins. Blackwell trains nurses for the Union army.

1864   Blackwell meets President Abraham Lincoln at the White House.

1869   Blackwell moves to England.

1895   Blackwell publishes her autobiography, *Pioneer Work in Opening the Medical Profession to Women.*

1907   Blackwell retires from the London School of Medicine for Women.

1910   Blackwell dies after suffering a stroke.

SOURCE NOTES

8 Elizabeth Blackwell, *Pioneer Work in Opening the Medical Profession to Women* (New York: Longmans, Green, 1895), 67.

10 Blackwell, 7.

12 Blackwell, 10.

14 Blackwell, 11.

15 Blackwell, 20.

15 Blackwell, 20–21.

16 Blackwell, 28.

17 Blackwell, 29.

20 Blackwell, 62.

22 Blackwell, 70.

24 Margaret Munro De Lancey, "Dr. Elizabeth Blackwell's Graduation—An Eyewitness Account," Internet Archive, accessed March 12, 2021, https://web.archive.org/web/20031212033218/http://academic.hws.edu/library/archives/pdfs/tripp.pdf.

26 Blackwell, *Pioneer Work*, 155.

30 Blackwell, 198.

32 Blackwell, 235.

33 "It Happened Here: Dr. Elizabeth Blackwell," NewYork-Presbyterian, accessed March 12, 2021, https://healthmatters.nyp.org/happened-dr-elizabeth-blackwell/.

40 "It Happened Here."

41 "Obituary," *British Medical Journal*, June 18, 2010, 1524, https://www.bmj.com/content/1/2581/1524.1.

SELECTED BIBLIOGRAPHY

Blackwell, Elizabeth. *Pioneer Work in Opening the Medical Profession to Women.* London: Longmans, Green, 1895.

De Lancey, Margaret Munro. "Dr. Elizabeth Blackwell's Graduation—An Eyewitness Account." Accessed March 12, 2021. https://web.archive .org/web/20031212033218/http://academic.hws.edu/library/archives /pdfs/tripp.pdf.

"It Happened Here: Dr. Elizabeth Blackwell." NewYork-Presbyterian. Accessed March 12, 2021. https://healthmatters.nyp.org/happened -dr-elizabeth-blackwell/.

Michals, Debra, ed. "Elizabeth Blackwell (1821–1910)." National Women's History Museum. Accessed March 12, 2021. https:// www.womenshistory.org/education-resources/biographies/elizabeth -blackwell.

LEARN MORE

BOOKS

Allman, Barbara. *The Most Influential Women in STEM*. New York: Rosen, 2019.

Lewis, Aura. *Spectacular Sisters: Amazing Stories of Sisters from Around the World*. New York: Quill Tree Books, 2021.

O'Brien, Cynthia. *Women Scientists Hidden in History*. New York: Crabtree, 2020.

WEBSITES

Britannica Kids: Elizabeth Blackwell
https://kids.britannica.com/kids/article/Elizabeth-Blackwell/400086

Kiddle: Vaccine Facts
https://kids.kiddle.co/Vaccine

National Park Service: Dr. Elizabeth Blackwell
https://www.nps.gov/people/dr-elizabeth-blackwell.htm

INDEX